GIANT
DINOSAURS!

The Sauropods

WORLD
BOOK

www.worldbook.com

For information about other World Book publications, visit our website at **www.worldbook.com** or call **1-800-WORLDBK (967-5325).**

For information about sales to schools and libraries, call **1-800-975-3250** (United States), or **1-800-837-5365** (Canada).

World Book, Inc.
180 North LaSalle Street
Suite 900
Chicago, IL 60601
USA

Amber Books Ltd.
74-77 White Lion Street
London N1 9PF
United Kingdom
www.amberbooks.co.uk

Library of Congress Cataloging-in-Publication Data

Giant dinosaurs : the Sauropods.
    p. cm. -- (Dinosaurs!)
    Summary: "An introduction to Sauropods, a group of dinosaurs that walked on four legs and that included the largest of all dinosaurs. Features include an original drawing of each dinosaur, fun facts, a glossary, and a list of additional resources"-- Provided by publisher.
    Includes index.
    ISBN 978-0-7166-0370-2
    1. Saurischia--Juvenile literature. I. World Book, Inc.
    QE862.S3G53 2013
    567.913--dc23
                                    2012016116
Dinosaurs!
ISBN 978-0-7166-0366-5 (4-volume set, hc.)
Giant Dinosaurs!: The Sauropods also available as:
ISBN 978-0-7166-3060-9 (e-book, EPUB3)

Printed in China by Toppan Leefung Printing Ltd., Guangdong Province
3rd printing September 2016

STAFF

Executive Committee

President
Jim O'Rourke
Vice President and Editor in Chief
Paul A. Kobasa
Vice President, Finance
Donald D. Keller
Vice President, Marketing
Jean Lin
Director, Human Resources
Bev Ecker

Editorial

Director, Digital & Print Content Development
Emily Kline
Editor, Digital & Print Content Development
Kendra Muntz
Associate Manager, Humanities
Kristina Vaicikonis
Editors
Will Adams
Nicholas Kilzer
Administrative Assistant
Ethel Matthews
Manager, Indexing Services
David Pofelski
Manager, Contracts & Compliance (Rights & Permissions)
Loranne K. Shields

Digital

Director, Digital Product Development
Erika Meller
Digital Product Manager
Lyndsie Manusos
Digital Product Coordinator
Matthew Werner

Manufacturing/Production

Manufacturing Manager
Sandra Johnson
Production/Technology Manager
Anne Fritzinger
Production Specialist
Curley Hunter
Proofreader
Nathalie Strassheim

Graphics and Design

Senior Art Director
Tom Evans
Senior Designer
Don Di Sante

Product development
Amber Books Ltd.
Authors
Per Christiansen and Chris McNab
Designer
Jerry Williams

Contents

Introduction 5

Prosauropods 8

Jurassic Sauropods 16

Cretaceous Sauropods 28

Dino Bite: Why Did Dinosaurs Become Extinct? 38

Where to Find Dinosaurs 40

Additional Resources 46

Index 47

Introduction

Paleontologist Fernando Novas of Argentina stands next to a fossil thighbone of the giant sauropod Antarctosaurus *(above)*. A reconstruction of a Diplodocus skeleton *(opposite)* dominates the Central Hall of the Natural History Museum in London.

Imagine standing in a forest about 100 million years ago as a mighty dinosaur tears great mouthfuls of leaves from branches high up in a tree. You are watching a sauropod *(SAWR-uh-PAHD)*, the largest of all the dinosaurs. This giant is far larger than any land animal alive today. In fact, some sauropods were the largest animals ever to live on land, reaching up to 130 feet (40 meters) long and weighing up to 85 tons (77 metric tons)!

Sauropods ate lots of plants every day. Their long necks allowed them to graze on ferns and shrubs near the ground or to reach leaves on the tallest trees. Sauropods also had small heads, long tails, and huge, deep chests and stomachs. Their whiplike tails and huge bodies helped to protect them from attackers. Some sauropods traveled in large herds for protection from huge meat-eating dinosaurs that roamed the land.

Scientists put sauropods and their ancestors into a larger group known as sauropodomorphs *(SAWR-uh-PAHD-uh-mawrphs)*. The earliest sauropodomorphs, called prosauropods, appeared about 230 million years ago, in the Triassic Period. During the Age of Dinosaurs, which lasted from about 252 million to 66 million years ago, sauropods spread to nearly every area of Earth. They were especially successful during the Jurassic Period, which lasted from about 201 million to 145 million years ago.

Earth went through great changes during the Age of Dinosaurs. In the beginning, a vast supercontinent called Pangaea *(pan-JEE-uh)* was surrounded by a great ocean. Pangaea broke apart over millions of years, and the continents began to drift toward the positions they occupy today. There also were great changes in plants and animals. Early in the Age of Dinosaurs, such seed plants as conifers, cycads, and ginkgoes were common. The first true mammals appeared, and crocodilians, frogs, insects, and lizards flourished. Flying reptiles called pterosaurs *(TEHR-uh-sawrz)* filled the skies. Plesiosaurs *(PLEE-see-uh-sawrz)* and other marine reptiles ruled the oceans. Later, flowering plants appeared and began to replace seed plants in some areas, helping insects and mammals to thrive. Birds arose from small meat-eating dinosaurs and soon spread around the world. The first snakes appeared, along with modern bony fish.

The Age of Dinosaurs

Period	Triassic	Jurassic	Cretaceous
Began	252 million years ago	201 million years ago	145 million years ago
Ended	201 million years ago	145 million years ago	66 million years ago
Major Events	Dinosaurs first appeared but did not become common until the end of this period.	Dinosaurs became the largest animals on land, reaching their greatest size.	A mass extinction at the end of this period killed off all the dinosaurs except some birds.

Dinosaurs first appeared during the Triassic Period. They became the largest, most successful land animals early in the Jurassic Period. The dinosaurs died out at the end of the Cretaceous Period. Together, these three periods make up the Mesozoic Era, the Age of Dinosaurs.

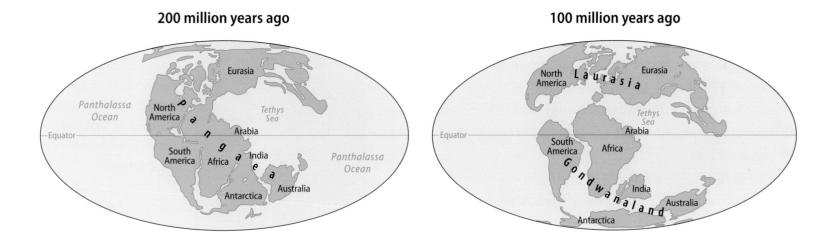

200 million years ago

Panthalassa Ocean

Eurasia

North America

Pangaea

Tethys Sea

Arabia

South America

Africa

India

Australia

Antarctica

Panthalassa Ocean

Equator

100 million years ago

North America

Laurasia

Eurasia

Tethys Sea

Arabia

South America

Africa

Gondwanaland

India

Australia

Antarctica

Equator

About 200 million years ago (*above left*) nearly all Earth's land formed a supercontinent scientists call Pangaea. It was surrounded by a vast ocean. Pangaea broke up into separate continents during the Age of Dinosaurs. By about 100 million years ago (*above right*), the continents had begun to drift toward the positions they occupy today.

Some dinosaurs flourished as conditions on Earth changed, while others struggled to adapt. By the Cretaceous Period, the sauropods had begun to die out. Scientists are not sure why. Sauropods all but disappeared from northern lands in the Cretaceous Period. But the breakup of Pangaea helped some sauropods to survive and even prosper in other areas. The last major group of sauropods, the supersized titanosaurs (*ty-TAN-nuh-sawrz*), thrived in what is now South America and other southern lands. These sauropods died out with the other dinosaurs about 65 million years ago.

Today, some scientists have different thoughts on what dinosaurs may have looked like. But, we can reconstruct the wonders of their world through the fossils they left behind.

Prosauropods

The prosauropods thrived at the beginning of the Age of Dinosaurs. They were the first dinosaurs to reach enormous sizes. There were many different kinds of prosauropods. Some were small, while others weighed more than a fully grown elephant.

The earliest prosauropods lived about 230 million years ago, in the middle of the Triassic Period. They were small animals that weighed no more than about 20 to 30 pounds (9 to 14 kilograms). Most walked on their long hind legs. Later, these animals grew so large that they had to walk on all fours.

Large prosauropods walked on all fours *(opposite)*, but most could stand up on their rear legs to reach food high in the trees *(left)*.

All prosauropods had sturdy bodies and long, thin necks with small heads. Many had large claws that may have been used to gather vegetation or to fight off predators. Prosauropods fed on the leaves of trees, or they ate ferns and herbs on the ground. Scientists think their teeth were used to bite off parts of plants—they were not shaped for chewing. These dinosaurs may have had a muscular stomach, much like the gizzard of a modern bird. They also swallowed stones that helped grind up plant matter into a digestible pulp.

For reasons unknown, the prosauropods died out early in the Jurassic Period, which began about 201 million years ago. However, scientists believe that certain prosauropods were the ancestors of sauropods. Along with other dinosaurs, these giants spread throughout the world.

Coloradisaurus

(kol-oh-RAHD-uh-SAWR-us)
Coloradisaurus walked on four
legs but stood on its rear legs
to feed on leaves from high
branches. It may have used
its clawed upper limbs to
defend itself.

Euskelosaurus

(yoo-skel-o-SAWR-us)
Euskelosaurus ate huge amounts
of *foliage* (leaves and stems) and
could strip a whole area of its
plant life. It was the first dinosaur
discovered in Africa, where its
fossils were found in 1863.

Melanorosaurus

(muh-LAN-or-o-SAWR-us)
Melanorosaurus had a large body
and sturdy limbs. It had spoon-
shaped teeth that were ideal for
raking leaves off branches.

Riojasaurus

(ree-OH-ha-SAWR-us)

A fully grown Riojasaurus could weigh up to 1,500 pounds (680 kilograms). Because it was so heavy, it could not stand on its back legs to feed, as other prosauropods did.

Plateosaurus

(PLATE-ee-o-SAWR-us)

Plateosaurus had a long neck and tail, features that were important for later sauropods. It had a large claw on its thumb to grab branches and pull them to its mouth.

FUN FACT

Dozens of Plateosaurus skeletons have been discovered. Because of this, scientists have learned a lot about their life history.

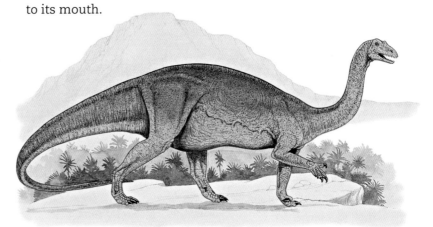

Mussaurus (moo-SAWR-us) lived in what is now South America about 220 million years ago. The first Mussaurus fossils discovered were those of babies. Mussaurus means "mouse lizard." This name refers to the dinosaur's young, which were only a bit larger than a mouse.

The discovery of Mussaurus young helped scientists learn how the dinosaurs reproduced and cared for their young. Mussaurus lived in groups of both adults and young. This arrangement would have provided some defense from meat-eating dinosaurs.

FACT O SAUR

Scientists think that many Mussaurus young were likely eaten before they reached adulthood.

Mussaurus adults were about 10 feet (3 meters) long, including the tail.

These relatively small prosauropods ate mostly low-growing ferns and other soft plants, which they bit off with their long, slender teeth.

Mussaurus had strong legs and could probably move quickly, running on all four limbs.

Ammosaurus

(am-o-SAWR-us)

Ammosaurus lived about 190 million years ago in what is now North America. A fossil Ammosaurus was found with the bones of another smaller dinosaur in its stomach area. Scientists think this prosauropod may have eaten both animals and plants.

Thecodontosaurus

(THEE-co-dont-oh-SAWR-us)

Thecodontosaurus was particularly quick because of its small size—it grew to only about 8 feet (2.5 meters) long. When threatened, it stood up and sprinted away.

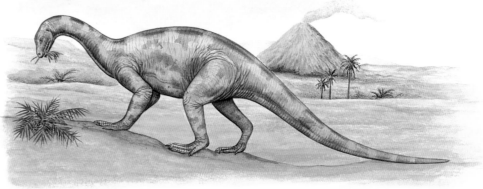

Anchisaurus

(an-key-SAWR-us)

A small dinosaur, Anchisaurus was about 7 feet (2 meters) in length. Like many plant-eating dinosaurs, Anchisaurus swallowed small stones that helped to grind up plant food in the dinosaur's stomach.

FUN FACT

Yunnanosaurus had up to 60 spoon-shaped teeth in its mouth. The teeth wore against each other as the dinosaur bit down, which kept the teeth sharp.

Yunnanosaurus

(YOU-nahn-o-SAWR-us)

Yunnanosaurus was well-equipped for gathering leaves from high in the trees. Its body was up to 60 feet (17 meters) long. It could stand on two legs and pull branches down with its claws.

The long, slender jaws were full of small, spoon-shaped teeth, suitable for biting off leaves. These teeth could not chew food.

Lufengosaurus broke up and ground its food with a muscular stomach, which contained stones, like the gizzards of many birds today.

Lufengosaurus

(loo-feng-o-SAWR-us) lived in what is now China about 200 million to 180 million years ago. It is one of the best-known of all prosauropods because so many of its fossils have been found. Lufengosaurus weighed up to 1,200 pounds (500 kilograms) and reached 20 feet (6.5 meters) long.

Lufengosaurus had powerful claws, especially on its thumbs.

FACT O SAUR

Like most prosauropods, Lufengosaurus had hind legs that were longer and thicker than its forelegs.

Jurassic Sauropods

Sauropods first appeared more than 200 million years ago, but scientists do not know much about their early history. They became more common during the early part of the Jurassic Period, which lasted from about 201 million to 145 million years ago. Sauropods soon spread all over the world.

All sauropods were large, sturdy animals with legs like columns—much like elephants today. They had long, slender necks, small heads, and very long tails. They all ate plants. However, we know that not all sauropods were alike. Some could lift their necks high into the air and probably grazed on the tops of trees like giraffes. Others fed close to the ground.

Scientists have found thousands of sauropod footprints all over the world, and these show that many of these dinosaurs lived and moved in herds. In the late Jurassic Period, sauropods were among the most common dinosaurs. Many different kinds of sauropods lived alongside one another, which suggests that they ate different kinds of plants. As the Jurassic Period ended, about 145 million years ago, many of the sauropods began to die out. Scientists are not sure why many sauropods disappeared at this time.

The fossilized skull of Camarasaurus *(below)*, a common sauropod dinosaur from North America, has many hollow spaces. Many sauropods had such holes, which helped to reduce the weight of the head at the end of the animal's long neck *(opposite)*.

Barapasaurus

(buh-RAH-pah-SAWR-us)
Hundreds of fossils found together at a single site in India suggest that Barapasaurus lived in herds. This living arrangement provided protection from meat-eating dinosaurs.

Vulcanodon

(vul-kan-oh-DON)
Vulcanodon was a mid-sized early sauropod known from fossils found in Africa. Scientists think it may represent a link between the prosauropods and the larger sauropods that appeared later.

Patagosaurus

(PAT-ah-goh-SAWR-us)
This early sauropod is known from fossils found in South America. It may be a close relative of Cetiosaurus.

Cetiosaurus

(SEAT-ee-oh-SAWR-us)

The name Cetiosaurus means "whale lizard." Scientists first thought that this dinosaur was a sea creature. It was later recognized as a sauropod. But it may have lived near water.

Kotasaurus

(KOHT-ah-SAWR-us)

Kotasaurus was an early sauropod known from fossils found in India. It has some features in common with prosauropods. It was about 30 feet (9 meters) long.

Brachiosaurus (brack-ee-uh-SAWR-us)

was a gigantic sauropod that looked somewhat like an enormous giraffe. It weighed up to 85 tons (77 metric tons) and stood more than 40 feet (12 meters) tall.

Brachiosaurus's head had a broad, flat snout and a large, dome-shaped ridge above the eyes. The nostrils opened from the ridge at the very top of the head, so this dinosaur did not have to stop eating to breathe.

FACT○SAUR

Brachiosaurus lived on the open plains of North America and Africa about 150 million years ago, feeding off the treetops.

Brachiosaurus was so tall that it could always find food high in the trees, even during *droughts* (unusually dry and rainless times). Other sauropods could not reach so high into the treetops.

Brachiosaurus's mouth was well-equipped to eat a lot of plants. It had up to 52 chisel-shaped teeth. The teeth were used to rake in leaves rather than for chewing.

Datousaurus

(dah-toe-SAWR-us)
Datousaurus had a body about 50 feet (15 meters) long, ending in a thin tail. Fossils of this creature are not found in groups, unlike those of many other sauropods. Therefore, scientists think this dinosaur may not have lived in herds.

FUN FACT

Different kinds of sauropods often lived in the same region. Each kind probably ate different plants, so they did not fight over food.

Brontosaurus

(BRON-toh-SAWR-us)
Brontosaurus lived in western North America. People used to think that it was the same animal as Apatosaurus, but scientists recently discovered that they are different dinosaurs. Its name means "thunder lizard."

Lapparentosaurus

(lah-pah-rent-oh-SAWR-us)

Lapparentosaurus is a sauropod dinosaur known from only a few fossils found on the island of Madagascar. No skull has been found, so scientists are not sure what it looked like.

Euhelopus

(you-HEL-oh-pus)

The name Euhelopus means "good marsh foot." Scientists gave the dinosaur this name because they thought it lived in marshy areas.

Diplodocus *(di-PLOD-o-kus)* was a huge sauropod that lived about 150 million years ago in what is now North America. Diplodocus could reach a length of 90 feet (27 meters). But it was slender in build. Diplodocus usually weighed only about 11 tons (10 metric tons), though some individuals may have grown much larger.

Diplodocus had 15 bones in its neck. These bones were hollow—if they had been solid, the dinosaur would not have been able to lift its own neck.

Scientists believe Diplodocus usually fed close to the ground, because its neck was not very flexible.

The tail of Diplodocus had more than 80 bones. It reached about 45 feet (14 meters) long, tapering to a thin tip. Diplodocus could have swung the tail like a whip to defend itself.

FACT◯SAUR

Diplodocus's teeth were long and thin and found only at the front of the mouth. The dinosaur tore at leaves rather than chewed them.

Shunosaurus (SHOO-no-SAWR-us)

lived in what is now China during the middle part of the Jurassic Period, about 170 million years ago. This plant-eating giant grew to about 33 feet (11 meters) in length and weighed about 10 tons (9.7 metric tons).

Shunosaurus had a club at the end of its long, strong tail. Some Shunosaurus tails even had spikes. An attacker whacked by this heavy weapon was likely to have been badly injured or even killed.

Unlike many sauropods, Shunosaurus had front and hind legs that were about the same length. As a result, its back was level with the ground.

FACT○SAUR

Paleontologists have unearthed several almost complete fossil skeletons of Shunosaurus. It is one of the best-known sauropods.

Apatosaurus

(ah-PAT-o-SAWR-us)

Apatosaurus lived in western North America. It was a mighty dinosaur, growing up to 80 feet (24 meters) long and weighing a hefty 33 tons (30 metric tons), slightly larger than its close relative Brontosaurus.

FUN FACT

The first skeleton of Apatosaurus displayed in a museum had the skull of a Camarasaurus. Many years passed before scientists discovered the mistake.

Camarasaurus

(kam-ah-rah-SAWR-us)

Camarasaurus is one of the best-known sauropods. Many of its fossils have been found in western North America. This dinosaur had hollow spaces in the bones of its neck and head, making them lighter and easier to move about.

Seismosaurus

(SIZE-moe-SAWR-us)
Seismosaurus means "earthquake lizard." It's a good name for this enormous dinosaur, which grew to about 150 feet (45 meters) long and weighed 85 tons (77 metric tons). It really may have caused the ground to rumble as it walked.

Omeisaurus

(OH-may-SAWR-us)
Old illustrations of Omeisaurus often show a club at the end of the tail. Scientists now think Omeisaurus lacked such a club and that its fossil remains were mixed up with the tail of a Shunosaurus.

Supersaurus (SUE-per-SAWR-us)

is known from only a few fossilized bones. The size of these bones suggests that this supersized dinosaur grew to a length of some 98 feet (30 meters) and a weight of 56 tons (51 metric tons).

FACT◯SAUR

The fossils of Supersaurus include bones that were once called Ultrasaurus. Only later did scientists realize the bones all belonged to one animal.

Like other large sauropods, Supersaurus probably spent most of each day eating. To save time and gather more food, Supersaurus did not chew its food. Instead, it tore leaves off trees and swallowed them whole.

Supersaurus had a very long neck and a very long tail. It was not the largest or heaviest sauropod, but it was one of the longest.

A single neckbone of Supersaurus stands more than 4 feet (1.2 meters) tall.

Cretaceous Sauropods

Sauropods were the largest, most common plant-eaters throughout much of the world for millions of years. Toward the end of the Jurassic Period, many died out. In the Cretaceous Period, which lasted from about 145 million to 66 million years ago, new kinds of plant-eating dinosaurs appeared and began competing with the remaining sauropods.

Sauropods had been common all over the world in the Jurassic Period, but in the Cretaceous Period almost all of them lived in the south, on the supercontinent scientists call Gondwana. This landmass was made up of present-day South America, Africa, Australia, and parts of Asia. The Cretaceous sauropods were also different from the Jurassic ones. Most of them belonged to a new group called the titanosaurs. They had sturdier bodies and legs than many of the Jurassic sauropods, but their necks and tails were shorter.

Many of the titanosaurs also developed armor. Their skin was covered with round, bony plates. These bony plates offered good protection from large, meat-eating dinosaurs. Titanosaurs were also protected by their great size. Most were simply too large for any meat-eater to take down. However, the young were vulnerable, and many were probably eaten before they were fully grown.

Nearly all Cretaceous sauropods, such as Jobaria from Africa *(opposite)*, and Rapetosaurus from Madagascar *(below)*, thrived in the Southern Hemisphere. Many Cretaceous sauropods were protected by armor made up of bony plates.

FUN FACT

Paleontologists have found preserved skin impressions of Pelorosaurus that show this sauropod was covered with *hexagonal* (six-sided) plates of tough skin.

Pelorosaurus

(pe-LOW-roh-SAWR-us)
Pelorosaurus was one of the first long-necked sauropods to be discovered. Its fossils were first found in the United Kingdom in 1849. It lived about 135 million years ago.

Aeolosaurus

(EE-oh-lo-SAWR-us)
Scientists think Aeolosaurus may have lived in herds, like many other sauropods. The herds would migrate to different feeding areas depending on the season.

Amargasaurus had two rows of spines running down its neck. Reaching as long as 20 inches (51 centimeters), these spines may have provided a defense against meat-eating dinosaurs.

Amargasaurus

(*uh-MARG-uh-SAWR-us*) lived in what is now South America about 125 million years ago. It was a relative of Diplodocus. Scientists think it probably fed on soft, low-growing ferns.

FACT○SAUR

The spikes of Amargasaurus may have served as protection, but some scientists think they may have been for show.

Amargasaurus had long and slender teeth that grew only at the front of the mouth. It had a rather short neck for a sauropod.

Antarctosaurus

(*ant-ARK-toe-SAWR-us*)
Antarctosaurus could stretch up and pull leaves off branches that were 20 feet (6.5 meters) above the ground. It had teeth only at the front of its mouth, so it was unable to chew food.

Hypselosaurus

(*HIP-sel-oh-SAWR-us*)
Hypselosaurus eggs were about 12 inches (30 centimeters) across. Scientists think that Hypselosaurus carefully positioned its eggs in the nest, because the eggs have been found in a tight clutch.

Argentinosaurus

(ahr-gen-TEEN-oh-SAWR-us), found in the South American country Argentina, was the largest land animal that ever lived. Although Argentinosaurus lived among gigantic meat-eating dinosaurs, it was at no risk of being hunted and eaten as an adult. This sauropod was simply too large to attack.

Argentinosaurus fossils were found in present-day Argentina, where it lived about 100 million years ago. It fed on the leaves of trees and shrubs. It needed to eat vast amounts of plant matter every day.

Argentinosaurus grew to a length of up to 135 feet (41 meters) and a weight of as much as 90 tons (82 metric tons)! Its thighbone alone was more than 8 feet (2.5 meters) long.

Argentinosaurus laid eggs on the ground. The young were quite small compared with the adults. Scientists think the adults did not provide care for their offspring.

33

Magyarosaurus

(MAG-yar-o-SAWR-us)

Magyarosaurus was a "dwarf" sauropod—it grew to "only" about 26 feet (8 meters) in length. Fossils of this dinosaur were found in what is now Romania in eastern Europe. Long ago, this region was a group of islands.

FUN FACT

Magyarosaurus was so small because it lived on islands. Large animals isolated on islands often become smaller over time.

Nemegtosaurus

(NAY-meg-toe-SAWR-us)

Little is known about Nemegtosaurus, fossils of which have been found in Mongolia, an Asian nation north of China. It had a very wide body, but its slender neck could reach into thick *foliage* (leaves) for feeding.

Neuquensaurus

(NOO-kwen-SAWR-us)
Neuquensaurus had skin that
was protected by bony plates.
This titanosaur is known from
71-million-year-old fossils found
in Argentina and Uruguay, in
South America.

Opisthocoelicaudia

(oh-PIS-tho-SEEL-ih-CAWD-ee-ah)
Opisthocoelicaudia was a stocky,
forest-dwelling dinosaur. The
name refers to its oddly shaped
tailbones, which were hollow.
The Opisthocoelicaudia stood on
its back legs and rested on its
tail, so it could reach high into
the trees to feed.

Quaesitosaurus

(kway-ZEET-oh-SAWR-us)
Quaesitosaurus is known only
from a single fossil skull found in
Mongolia. It was a large sauropod
with unusually large ear openings.
It may have had keen hearing.

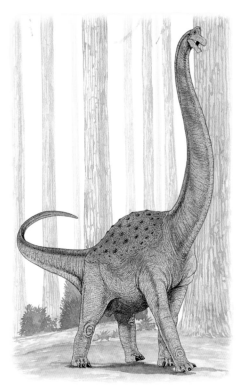

Rapetosaurus

(rah-PETE-oh-SAWR-us)
Rapetosaurus is one of the last dinosaurs to develop on Earth. Fossils of this dinosaur, found in Madagascar, are only about 70 million years old.

Alamosaurus

(al-uh-moe-SAWR-us)
Alamosaurus could grow up to 70 feet (21 meters) long. Scientists think this dinosaur roamed the land in huge herds.

Saltasaurus (SALT-ah-SAWR-us)

was a long-necked sauropod covered in armor. It lived in what is now South America about 80 million years ago. It was about 40 feet (12 meters) long and weighed 3 to 4 tons (2.7 to 3.6 metric tons).

Hard, bony plates were embedded in the skin of the dinosaur's back. This would have made Saltasaurus difficult to attack.

No complete skull of a Saltasaurus has been found, but it probably had long, peglike teeth to strip leaves off branches.

Like other titanosaurs, Saltasaurus was powerfully built and had sturdy legs, with a wide, plump body.

DINO BITE

Why Did Dinosaurs Become Extinct?

For about 160 million years, dinosaurs were the largest and most successful animals on Earth. Then, about 66 million years ago, they disappeared. They died in a mass *extinction* (die off) that affected much of life on Earth. In fact, all animals that weighed more than about 50 pounds (23 kilograms) died out. Many smaller animals and some plants also became extinct.

Scientists have developed many theories to explain this extinction. However, since the early 1980's, scientists have uncovered strong evidence that it was caused by the collision of a large asteroid with Earth. (An asteroid is a rocky or metallic object in space smaller than a planet.) The asteroid was at least 6 miles (10 kilometers) across and was traveling at tremendous speed when it struck near what is now Mexico.

The asteroid impact was terrible. It created a crater about 112 miles (180 kilometers) across. It threw billions of tons of dust and *debris* (other matter) into the atmosphere. Hot debris falling back to the surface may have caused huge fires worldwide. The clouds of smoke and debris would have blocked sunlight from reaching the surface of Earth for many months. The darkened skies likely caused land temperatures to drop below freezing across much of the world. Although the seeds and roots of many plants were able to survive under such harsh conditions, the leaves and other parts of the plants died. Without plants to eat, dinosaurs such as sauropods could not survive. As the plant-eaters died, so did the meat-eating dinosaurs that fed on them.

The sauropods died out with other dinosaurs about 66 million years ago. Scientists have developed a number of theories to explain this mass extinction.

While most scientists now agree that the asteroid was the primary cause of the mass extinction, some scientists believe that other factors may also have played a role. At this time, there were giant volcanic eruptions in what is now India. These eruptions created huge lava beds called the Deccan Traps. These lava beds covered about 200,000 square miles (500,000 square kilometers). The lava beds have cooled to volcanic stone. The beds are more than 1 mile (1.6 kilometers) thick in places. Such enormous eruptions would have released large volumes of gas that caused rapid climate change.

Other factors may also have contributed to the mass extinction. Some scientists argue that dinosaurs were already in decline when the asteroid struck. In the late Cretaceous Period, flowering plants had spread to many areas, which may have benefited mammals and other animals at the expense of dinosaurs. But other scientists reject the argument that dinosaurs were in decline.

In truth, scientist still cannot explain why some living things survived the mass extinction while others died out. In fact, most scientists now believe that birds arose from small, meat-eating dinosaurs. Why did certain birds survive the extinction, when other birds and dinosaurs became extinct? Scientists continue to study and debate the causes of the mass extinction that devastated life on Earth about 66 million years ago.

Where to Find Dinosaurs

Museums in the United States

ARIZONA

The Arizona Museum of Natural History
53 North Macdonald
Mesa, Arizona 85201

Theropods, sauropods, and other dinosaurs rule at Dinosaur Hall and on Dinosaur Mountain.

CALIFORNIA

Natural History Museum of Los Angeles County
900 Exposition Boulevard
Los Angeles, California 90007

After you explore the fossils and skeletons in Dinosaur Hall, get a behind-the-scenes look at how the exhibits are made in the Dino Lab.

University of California Museum of Paleontology
1101 Valley Life Sciences Building
Berkeley, California 94720

Many of this museum's exhibits are viewable online as well as in person.

COLORADO

The Denver Museum of Nature & Science
2001 Colorado Boulevard
Denver, Colorado 80205

Dynamic re-creations of ancient environments as well as hands-on fossils tell the story of prehistoric life.

Dinosaur National Monument
4545 Hwy 40, Dinosaur National Monument
Dinosaur, Colorado 81610

Dinosaur National Monument is located in both Colorado and Utah. Its world-famous Carnegie Dinosaur Quarry, home to about 1,500 dinosaur fossils, is on the Utah side.

CONNECTICUT

Dinosaur State Park
400 West Street
Rocky Hill, Connecticut 06067

Here you will find one of the largest dinosaur track sites in North America. Visitors can also explore the Arboretum, which contains more than 200 species of plants—many dating back to prehistoric eras.

CONNECTICUT *continued*

The Yale Peabody Museum of Natural History
170 Whitney Avenue
New Haven, Connecticut 06511

Don't miss the Great Hall of Dinosaurs with its famous "Age of Reptiles" mural—one of the largest in the world.

Dinosaur National Monument
Dinosaur, Colorado

GEORGIA

The Fernbank Museum of Natural History

767 Clifton Road NE

Atlanta, Georgia 30307

See a Giganotosaurus and other dinosaurs in the Giants of the Mesozoic exhibit.

ILLINOIS

The Chicago Children's Museum at Navy Pier

700 East Grand Avenue

Chicago, Illinois 60611

Kids of all ages can explore a re-creation of an actual dinosaur excavation, where you can search for bones in an excavation pit.

The Discovery Center Museum

711 North Main Street

Rockford, Illinois 61103

Visitors will enjoy the simulated dinosaur dig at this children's museum.

The Field Museum

1400 South Lake Shore Drive

Chicago, Illinois 60605

Chicago's Field Museum is home to Sue, the largest and most complete Tyrannosaurus rex skeleton ever discovered.

INDIANA

The Dinosphere at the Children's Museum of Indianapolis

3000 North Meridian Street

Indianapolis, Indiana 46208

Experience the world of the dinosaurs with family digs, fossil preparation, and sensory exhibits.

MAINE

The Maine Discovery Museum

74 Main Street

Bangor, Maine 04401

Young visitors to this children's museum can explore the world of paleontology at the museum's new Dino Dig exhibit.

MASSACHUSETTS

The Museum of Science, Boston

1 Science Park

Boston, Massachusetts 02114

A 23-foot- (7-meter-) long Triceratops specimen, found in the Dakota Badlands, is just one of the fascinating fossils on display here.

MICHIGAN

The University of Michigan Museum of Natural History

1109 Geddes Avenue

Ann Arbor, Michigan 48109

Michigan's largest collection of prehistoric specimens can be found in the Museum of Natural History's rotunda and galleries.

The Field Museum,
Chicago, Illinois

The American Museum of Natural History, New York City

MINNESOTA

The Science Museum of Minnesota
120 West Kellogg Boulevard
St. Paul, Minnesota 55102

Do some hands-on fossil exploration at the Paleontology Lab, then get inside the jaws of a giant T. rex to simulate its mighty bite!

MONTANA

The Museum of the Rockies
600 West Kagy Blvd
Bozeman, Montana 59717

This museum's Siebel Dinosaur Complex houses one of the largest collections of dinosaur fossils in the world.

NEW MEXICO

The New Mexico Museum of Natural History and Science
1801 Mountain Road NW
Albuquerque, New Mexico 87104

The exciting Timetracks exhibit covers the Triassic, Jurassic, and Cretaceous periods.

NEW YORK

The American Museum of Natural History
Central Park West at 79th Street
New York, New York 10024

This museum's famous Fossil and Dinosaur halls house nearly 1 million specimens.

NORTH CAROLINA

North Carolina Museum of Natural Sciences
11 West Jones Street
Raleigh, North Carolina 27601

Home to Willo the Thescalosaurus, an Acrocanthosaurus, and four fossilized whales.

PENNSYLVANIA

The Academy of Natural Sciences of Drexel University
1900 Benjamin Franklin Parkway
Philadelphia, Pennsylvania 19103

Impressive skeletons of massive dinosaurs stalk Drexel's Dinosaur Hall. Visitors can also visit the fossil lab to learn how fossils are prepared and studied.

The Carnegie Museum of Natural History
4400 Forbes Avenue
Pittsburgh, Pennsylvania 15213

The Dinosaurs in the Their Time exhibit features scientifically accurate re-creations of environments from the Age of Dinosaurs.

SOUTH DAKOTA

The Children's Museum of South Dakota
521 4th Street
Brookings, South Dakota 57006

Meet Mama and Max, a pair of full-sized animatronic T. rex dinosaurs, and try your hand at a dinosaur dig.

TENNESSEE

The Creative Discovery Museum
321 Chestnut Street
Chattanooga, Tennessee 37402
The Creative Discovery Museum's Excavation Station lets young visitors dig their own dinosaur bones.

TEXAS

The Houston Museum of Natural Science
5555 Hermann Park Drive
Houston, Texas 77030
The world-class Hall of Paleontology includes more than 30 dinosaurs and many other prehistoric creatures in "action" poses.

UTAH

The Natural History Museum of Utah
301 Wakara Way
Salt Lake City, Utah 84108
The paleontology collections at Utah's Natural History Museum include more than 30,000 specimens.

VIRGINIA

The Virginia Museum of Natural History
21 Starling Avenue
Martinsville, Virginia 24112
Detailed models and interactive features accompany the dinosaur exhibits.

WASHINGTON, D.C.

The National Museum of Natural History—Smithsonian Institution
10th Street & Constitution Avenue NW
Washington, D.C. 20560
Visit the National Fossil Hall—free of charge—to come face-to-face with dinosaurs, fossil mammals, and fossil plants.

WYOMING

The Wyoming Dinosaur Center
110 Carter Ranch Road
Thermopolis, Wyoming 82443
The combined museum and dig site offers daylong digs for visitors of all ages.

The Carnegie Museum
of Natural History,
Pittsburgh, Pennsylvania

Museums in Canada

ALBERTA

The Royal Tyrrell Museum
1500 North Dinosaur Trail
Drumheller, Alberta T0J 0Y0, Canada
Tyrannosaurus rex, Triceratops, Quetzalcoatlus (a pterodactyloid), and many other fossils can be found here.

ONTARIO

The Canadian Museum of Nature
240 McLeod Street
Ottawa, Ontario, Canada
Explore the lives—and the eventual extinction—of the dinosaurs in the Fossil Gallery.

The London Children's Museum
21 Wharncliffe Road South
London, Ontario N6J 4G5, Canada
The Dinosaur Gallery includes demonstrations, fossil casts, and replicas of many dinosaurs from the Jurassic Period.

The Royal Ontario Museum
100 Queen's Park
Toronto, Ontario, M5S 2C6, Canada
These exhibits feature dinosaurs and other fossils from the Jurassic and Cretaceous periods.

QUEBEC

The Redpath Museum
859 Sherbrooke Street West
Montreal, Quebec, Canada
Learn about the animals that roamed prehistoric Quebec as well as about many types of dinosaur.

Museums in the United Kingdom

The Dinosaur Museum
Icen Way, Dorchester
Dorset, DT1 1EW, United Kingdom
Highlights include kid-friendly, hands-on computer displays, dinosaur skeletons, and a wide range of fossils.

The National Museum of Scotland
Chambers Street
Edinburgh, EH1 1JF, United Kingdom
Allosaurus and Triceratops skeletons are part of a prehistory exhibit, along with dinosaur footprints and a "dino dig" for young visitors.

The Natural History Museum
Cromwell Road, London SW7 5BD
The elaborate dinosaur gallery includes four animatronic dinosaurs.

Oxford University Museum of Natural History
Parks Road, Oxford,
OX1 3PW, United Kingdom
The outstanding collection of dinosaur fossils and skeletons includes a Camptosaurus, Cetiosaurus, Eustreptospondylus, Iguanodon, Lexovisaurus, Megalosaurus, and a Metriacanthosaurus.

The Royal Tyrrell Museum
Drumheller, Canada

Museums in Australia

The Australian Museum
6 College Street, Sydney
New South Wales 2010, Australia

A permanent dinosaur exhibit features high-tech interactive displays, animatronic dinosaurs, and a paleontology lab that is open to young visitors.

The Melbourne Museum
11 Nicholson St. Carlton
Victoria, 3053, Australia

A kid-friendly Dinosaur Walk exhibition brings the prehistoric world to life.

The National Dinosaur Museum
Gold Creek Road and Barton Highway
Nicholls, Australia Capital Terrority 2913, Australia

Home to the largest permanent display of dinosaur and other prehistoric fossil material in Australia.

Museums in New Zealand

The Canterbury Museum
Christchurch Central, Christchurch 8013, New Zealand

The Geology gallery features fossils and an introduction to the fearsome marine reptiles of New Zealand's prehistory.

The Australian Museum
Sydney, Australia

Additional Resources

Books

Dinosaur Discovery: Everything You Need to Be a Paleontologist
by Christopher McGowan and Erica Lyn Schmidt
(Simon and Schuster Books for Young Readers, 2011)

Activities and experiments show readers how paleontologists examine ancient fossils.

Dinosaur Mountain: Digging into the Jurassic Age
by Deborah Kogan Ray (Frances Foster Books/Farrar, Straus, Giroux, 2010)

Follow fossil expert Earl Douglass on his 1908 hunt for dinosaur bones, which led to the discovery of several amazing skeletons.

Dinosaurs: The Most Complete, Up-to-Date Encyclopedia for Dinosaur Lovers of All Ages
by Thomas R. Holtz and Luis V. Rey (Random House, 2007)

A reference guide to all things dinosaur, from fossil hunting to evolution.

How the Dinosaur Got to the Museum
by Jessie Hartland (Blue Apple Books, 2013)

Diplodocus is unearthed in Utah and then sent to a dinosaur exhibit at the Smithsonian Museum in Washington, D.C.

The Ultimate Dinopedia: The Most Complete Dinosaur Reference Ever
by Don Lessem (National Geographic, 2010)

This beautifully illustrated and fact-filled dinosaur reference covers almost every dinosaur ever discovered.

Movies

Bizarre Dinosaurs
(National Geographic, 2009)

Paleontologists lead you on a tour of some of the strangest dinosaurs to ever walk the Earth.

Dinosaur Collection
(Discovery-Gaiam, 2011)

Computer-animated simulations paint a vivid picture of dinosaurs and their world.

Dinosaurs Unearthed
(National Geographic, 2007)

Watch the examination of a mummified dinosaur for a new understanding of how dinosaurs looked, moved, and lived.

Index

A

Aeolosaurus, 30
Age of Dinosaurs, 5-8
Alamosaurus, 36
Amargasaurus, 31
Ammosaurus, 13
Anchisaurus, 14
Antarctosaurus, 5, 32
Apatosaurus, 21, 25
Argentinosaurus, 33
asteroid collision, 38-39

B

Barapasaurus, 18
birds, 39
Brachiosaurus, 20
Brontosaurus, 21, 25

C

Camarasaurus, 16-17, 25
Cetiosaurus, 19
Coloradisaurus, 10
Cretaceous Period, 6-7,
    28-37, 39

D

Datousaurus, 21
Deccan Traps, 39

dinosaurs, 4-7, 40-45;
    extinction of, 7, 38-39.
    See also sauropods
Diplodocus, 4-5, 23, 26, 31

E

Euhelopus, 22
Euskelosaurus, 10
extinction of dinosaurs, 7,
    38-39

G

Giganotosaurus, 33
Gondwana, 28

H

Hypselosaurus, 32

J

Jobaria, 28-29
Jurassic Period, 5-6, 8, 16-28

K

Kotasaurus, 19

L

Lapparentosaurus, 22
Lufengosaurus, 15

M

Magyarosaurus, 34
Melanorosaurus, 10
Mesozoic Era. *See* Age
    of Dinosaurs
museums, 40-45
Mussaurus, 12

N

Nemegtosaurus, 34
Neuquensaurus, 35
Novas, Fernando, 5

O

Omeisaurus, 26
Opisthocoelicaudia, 35

P

Pangaea, 5-7
Patagosaurus, 18
Pelorosaurus, 30
Plateosaurus, 11
prosauropods, 5, 8-15

Q

Quaesitosaurus, 35

R

Rapetosaurus, 29, 36
Riojasaurus, 11

S

Saltasaurus, 37
sauropodomorphs, 5
sauropods, 5-8; Cretaceous,
    28-37; extinction of, 7,
    38-39; Jurassic, 16-27
Seismosaurus, 26
Shunosaurus, 24
Supersaurus, 27

T

Thecodontosaurus, 13
titanosaurs, 7, 28
Triassic Period, 5-8

U

Ultrasaurus, 27

V

volcanic eruptions, 39
Vulcanodon, 18, 19

Y

Yunnanosaurus, 14

Photo Credits